MW01566871

This Journal belongs to :

....

Made in the USA
Las Vegas, NV
24 March 2021

20100062R00056